ACKNOWLEDGMENTS

Thank you to the editors of the following journals/broadcasts where these
poems appeared, sometimes in an earlier version:

32 Poems: "The Statues of Rome"; *Timberline Review*: "Adjacent to the
Vatican"; *Salamander*: "A Strand of Hair Curled Like a Nautilus on a Page
of Rumi"; *Cimarron Review*: "Thinking of Adolph Gotlieb's *Drift* While I
Mow the Grass"; *Naugatuck Review*: "Province Lands", *Indolent Books Press*:
"At Stop & Shop After the Election, 2016"; *Crab Creek Review*: "A Strand of
Hair on My T-Shirt's Peace Sign"; *Lily Poetry Review*: "Again, I Take to the
Trees"; *Mom Egg Review*: "At Eighteen"; *Literary Mama*: "Lost and Found";
Ruminate: "This Hole is as Hopeful as Any"; *Sugar House Review*: "My
Greatest Story"; *Nixes Mate Review*: "What I Want to Say Driving Home
After My Mother's Check-Up"; *Passager Books*: "You Chose Pain"; *Blue
Mountain Review*: "Reconsidering the Oyster"; WCAI Poetry Sunday: "Early
Morning Swim at Ballston Beach"; *cagibi*: "Early Morning Swim at Ballston
Beach," "Nipple Reconstruction or No Nipple Reconstruction"; *Cape Cod
Times*: "College Break".

Publisher: Leah Maines
Editor: Christen Kincaid
Cover Art: *Girl Without a Shirt* copyright Michael E. Jones 2019
Author Photo: Sarah Lain
Cover Design: Martha McCollough

Printed in the USA on acid-free paper.
Order online: www.finishinglinepress.com
also available on amazon.com

Author inquiries and mail orders:
Finishing Line Press
P. O. Box 1626
Georgetown, Kentucky 40324
U. S. A.

Table of Contents

( )

"The test of a first-rate intelligence is the ability to hold two opposed ideas in mind at the same time and still retain the ability to function."
~ *F. Scott Fitzgerald*

for my parents, Don & Rachel,
my children Megan & Owen,

and for Michael, always.

"Today, let us swim wildly, joyously in gratitude."
~ *Rumi*

On Becoming a Lady

I take it from the bucket,
loose body, gray silk

in its juice. I eat it
bare, on ice with a lemon.

The slip of it
kindles a craving

for the days I'd run
the street without a shirt,

another pirate.
Girl exposed.

Now, when I run,
a scrap of fabric protects me.

From what exactly?
My breasts stay strapped,

though my nipples covet,
stand erect—improper

little battle cries.
Sitting at the table,

legs properly crossed,
I let the briny flesh slide.

Girl Without a Shirt

poems by

Christine Jones

Finishing Line Press
Georgetown, Kentucky

Girl Without a Shirt

Again, I Take to the Trees

A quilt of rooftops,

a silo,

a boy on a blue Schwinn.

Also, a cardinal,

and three holes chewed from a slim leaf.

( )

To be tall is to overhear
the world muttering,
like the grain faintly churning,
a feeling confessing itself to itself.

( )

Such testing admission, here,
beneath the wind's cowl,

in the face of daggering boughs.
Even the days of calm swaying can stagger.

( )

I first took to the trees as a girl;
pestering each limb to consider me. Fell.

There are heights, and there are heights.

On that occasion, I landed on
the only skein of grass the grove offered.
The ground forgave.

A Strand of Hair Curled Like a Nautilus on a Page of Rumi

When lifted, it surrenders

    like a dervish

        in slow motion.   I place

the strand back   as I found it,

    believing nothing is   happenstance.

Logarithms evolve

    into a sunflower,

a cyclone,   a galaxy.

    Although changed, I remain the same,

        eadem mutata resurgo,

            like a high-wire artist

    walking infinitely   along the spiral depths

    of a fiddlehead fern,

a grapevine's tendril,

        a wave's curl.

At Walden

I'm stuck in Thoreau's frumpy kettle
pond, swallowing pollen.

It keeps me from saying
all the mean things I say.

I attract more allergies every day,
but in dreams, when the bees come

I motion for help. They know
how to start things over,

seeding me until the pond swells
into a forgiving ocean, and I find myself

far from any middle. I see shore lights
stuttering, and a soft lift of salt

brings me to the edge of that cold
complication; that summit

where a good hurt begins.

This Hole is as Hopeful as Any

Claw at the bight's grain.
Still that something burrows farther
from you. More holes, the clams'
fledgling mouths expose themselves
as tide gnaws the water.
Gnats swarm; gray snow
rearranging itself, unmoved
in its moving. They are
disruption, tacks mapping
the body—here you are
trekking fistful through
wet holes collapsing;
here you are radiant; and here
you are sensing the blue heron
standing one-legged, nearby
in the marsh, conserving its heat.

Swimming, Dark Like

The sun sends a green light
across the surface, spiraling
as if proclaiming a ghost ship's approaching.
And there's Anne Sexton,
posing in her white one piece.

Waves pull. Kicking
against her darkness—
that lyrical well
she dug deeper
for what sip she thought
would revive her;

the figurative cave
she clawed at with
her sharpest finger, mining
for a light to find her;

the two portraits (a smile like her mother's)
on opposite walls in Gloucester.

Swimming, swimming. Brilliancy—
dark, wet as the cormorant's feathers, the
right whale's back, iridescent
as this broken dusk.

DaVinci's Treatise *On Painting*

An enameled bowl on a table covered
by gold cloth with frayed tassels
folded into the corner of the frame,

and in the bowl,
three content apples, two
pears and a plum.

Hear the skin
split, taste the juice

of an oblong plum
mashed to the ground,
bubbled with sugar,
shrouded with fat ants.

The plum shifts,
grows to a hibiscus,
an osprey, a crab that burrows—

wanting you to find
its mad flower, its wingéd mate,
its pith in purple ash.

Adjacent to the Vatican

Having come from the Sistine Chapel,
you're sipping espresso
in St. Peter's Square, and there,
on the Basilica's steps, a girl

begging, plastic cup and a Lab
at her feet. You stop, pat the pup,
admire the girl's purple hair, the shark
penned on her inner left arm.

Give her a euro, then you're off
for that gelato, tasting much like it does
at home, across the dirty pavers,
past the Bernini fountain, down Via Virgilio.

Not even the Pope could explain
better the darks and lights of Rome
where vendors' noisemakers rip
the air, the trinity, or the way God
is supposed to enter us all. Instead

it's the girl's skin, inked blue,
the way the tip of the shark's tail curls
in the bend of her elbow, and how
when she straightens her arm,

you see it rise.

The Statues of Rome

Every war destructs
the already destructed

torso found in a field,
or a hill, or the hall
of a great museum.

The schismed core
of alabaster is what remains,

what offers a nipple,
stone-still,

to the dead, to
the living who bleed,

and the living who try to feed,
and be fed.

At Stop & Shop After the Election, 2016

This day, muted, as though under a salon's
dryer hood. Its white-noise-dome moves
with me wherever I go. I wander

the aisles, bump into the free-standing
display of the now fruitier Fruit Loops.
I fiddle with each jar, each cardboard box;

dither, shake, consider every priced ounce.
I shuffle past neon-colored cans of
cat food, thirteen brands of pickles, so many

kinds of chips, I can never decide.
On the magazine rack, *Women's World* pushes
against today's headlines, while my red grapes roll

on the conveyor. At the exit, a bag
in each fist, I'm chewing my new pack of
gum from the point-of-purchase shelf, waiting

before the whale-mouthed door opens.

Psalm for the Page Turner

I knelt, unforgiving, unforgiven,
years ago, composed
entirely of dissonance. I was
boneless in a pew, folding
my bulletin, a crooked fan, mouthing
a creed I pretended to know. Faith

is what the man in a robe called it,
but I'd washed his dishes in the rector's house,
knew he was messy like the rest of us.

And my aunt, in her convent, enveloped
in her starchy habit, meant well
enough with her pewter saints
in her small plain cell—too small

for me. But here, this lady
in navy slacks, her finger poised
in midair, formal as Adam awaiting
God's breath. Such attention.

How she leans in precisely
when the last note of each page
is played. Small rapture
of silhouette against the rose
mosaic porthole swells;

crested voices, taste of bread—
the wine lingers.

Warning Before Jumping from a Cliff Above the Amalfi Coast

Step too big, and the air
jackknifes you; the water,

hardening to asphalt, bloodies
your thighs. Step too small,

and your arms, pinned straight,
arrow deeper than your breath

allows. But wait, and you
might not leap, missing

the water's more giving slap—the gasp
tailed by the swift bruise of air.

What Do We, Failing, Know of Virtue?

The artist abandons her son;
makes a painting ten feet tall.

She stores the canvas in the barn,
behind her portraits of noblemen and ladies,
her muddied paintings of Medusa.

I'm a mother. I've judged her, too.

She faces it backward, pressed
against her sketch of giant cherubs
dangling naked people. Flesh of hips,

thighs tensed, the painted woman rides
a sizable horse to a vanishing point

of black diamonds. How swift the figure
turning from the boy riding a runnable horse

galloping toward her. She's lying
when she says she has no regrets. Yet
it's become her official position; like the hair

she frets loose from the painted woman's bun,
the strict pull of the reins the figure holds.

Every Pomegranate a Story

Quartered, the fruit
unveils a wasp nest.

Its calloused clusters, blisters
ready to weep, tumble,

with a nudge from a thumb.
They barely fill a ramekin,

but still their sadness stains.
Persephone, of course,

and Demeter; how their sour
myth rushes the tongue,

but there are only so many ways
a woman sorrows at her arrival.

Each aril, a chapter.

I Bit Her

My daughter laughs
when I tell her the story.

Still, I see those red indentations.
How strange that mark; the same
split shape of a woman's kiss.

I didn't break the skin.

But I was late for work,
and while yoking her into
the car seat, wrangling with
the stuck and twisted stained
straps, she went full-on-animal,
flapping like a tuna
on a wet deck.

When she caught me
with a left hook,
I bit her flailing arm. Shock

shook us both from our
wailing, woke my list
of most liable worsts.

She forgives me
by not remembering.

You Chose Pain

over the epidural,

resisted the needle, past the point
of option. Now, your hips

display your banquet
of all that is not pretty.

You're beyond the Versailles
of a woman's public body,

its topiary, the rational order
of "First comes love.

Then comes marriage."
There sits a sparrow

on the labor room's sill,
pruning its breast.

It knows you, too,
are one of nature's devices.

When the child crowns,
what you see is guileless,

misshapened, milk consuming
you with its selfish potential,

like the child who attaches,
the child who lets go.

During the Eclipse

for Michael

It's most evident we're orbiting,

When I look at you, you're fixed,
until I blink

and you've moved toward the driveway.

I blink again, and there

you're under the dogwood.

This deviant moon proves nothing
escapes the world's revolution;

not the tinnitus of crickets, not the garlic scent
of your collar, or my uncertainty,
wondering how we got here, together,
on this front lawn. Many nights,

this lunar body hole-punches
darkness, a perfect escape route,
but not tonight. Tonight,

when you tilt me just so,

the evening rights itself.

But Will You Stay?

We fuck to the thump of the dryer,
in the basement, on the concrete floor.
Upstairs, the oven is heating our dinner.

This is the home we've made together.
It's perfect. I'm holding you here,
but are we too fat on persimmons,

it's over? There's no stopping it—
such leaving, like sleeveless trees in winter.

I'll be a trunk, a valise of centuries,
lined with the eons of women who, too,
tried to keep someone like you near.

My body, my barrow. My love,
your laundry's done. You're free
to go. But not before I drape this towel,

like a clean sail, across your chest. There,
you feel warmer now.

At Eighteen

But Will You Stay

You've learned the word *chrysalism*
from the *Dictionary of Obscure Sorrows;*

also, what a mother feels.

I believe you, daughter,
when you tell me you're sad;

and when you say you won't wait
until you're dead to be famous.

But for today, I'm content
when you discover the vase

of wild asters painted beneath
Van Gogh's *Three Pairs of Shoes.*

Before My Daughter Loves Her Virginity

When you call, I think of the trout,
copper-sequined, near the slip,

giving itself away
below the lake's meniscus.

( )

I know you meant to plunge, but didn't
when once you streaked,
along Cahoon Hollow's freckled shore.

I can see you pacing, considering
the slowed metronome of surf, Cassiopeia
shifting overhead, the night pawing at your wishes.

You never liked getting wet; the girl
afraid of her own delight, who
wouldn't ride a bike without braking.

My collector of rhodonite, I want you to trust
the rush, even when it swamps all
you've organized in your small, precise tins.

( )

My first time, I was sick with flu,
fevered, then later, confused
by the tranquil bobcat; content, sated, reflected

in my room's every mirrored surface;
the window, the water glass,
the bureau's brass knobs.

( )

If only a girl's body in the world
would stay simple, natural as
the widening of her hips.

Desire is explicable, but not
its fullness, how it leaves you
teetering in a bamboo hammock,
the mosquito-net teeming.

( )

You don't tell me about him,
but I hope he adores the rim
of your waist, still soft with baby flesh.

You don't tell me who he is,
but I want him to notice your faded lisp,
the vague trace of your overbite.

You don't tell me his name,
but I ask him to protect
your chin's fin-shaped scar.

()

( )

Province Lands

Here the dunes are fleshy
          and the troubled grasses bend

in that way you and I
          are so inclined, making love

inside this low-cut valley. A chopper,
          missioning, too, in this state park,

passes over our kindling. We reek
          of quartz and phosphorus.

Some manage to keep desire's
          matchstick shoved in a damp pocket,

while others strike its same burnt head
          in search of the flare again.

But we, we swaddle our fire, waiting
          for pink soot to settle

in a cave where little gods
          are casting their votes.

You're Made a Goddess

when she's born. A terrible thing.
You find a city you can't take, a girl

you can't shape into your likeness.
The scratches on your breastplate

are remnants, like the rivers in her palm
found by the seer at the village fair,

forming a star, proof she's all things
the heavens sense: a vole in the garden bed,

a gray seal's shadow. Even Orion, hunting
the skies nightly, can't get a mark on her.

A Strand of Hair on My T-Shirt's Peace Sign

looks like a length of tinsel,
and I'm five again, under the Christmas tree,
circling the cowgirl outfit from the Sears catalogue.

      Violent as any child, I wanted
      the plastic six-shooter,
                         yet later,
      wouldn't let my son have a toy gun.
      Instead, he got a telescope,
                a bin of wooden blocks.

      Still, he used a stick, or broom
      to take his shot. Played dead;

      immortality, a kid's privilege.

He wanted to be a scientist,
said he'd make happy things.

Today, he wants
to be a businessman, buy a house
with three chimneys, vote. Says,
      he'll *need a gun*
to protect his future wife, two kids.

My son now lives with the ranks of men.
This strand that matches his;

      I let him go.

In the Wake of Divorce

At the YMCA, you found me, a moth in a basin.
Took me to the ocean to teach me; edgeless pool
strewn with sargassum, also small jellies—another
kind of wreckage. I palmed each one, committed
to the sting. Now, years later, I find the paper napkin
you leave on my dashboard, its jumbled words a puzzle
more complex than three horseshoe crabs mating,
revealing, like water refracting off a cormorant's wing.

While Stingy Rain Whittles an Afternoon

The mother returns the jar
        to the highest shelf. Unopened.

She believed the object simple:
        for each kind act, a sweet.

On the first day, the girl fed her gerbil,
        and the boy cleaned its cage. She helped

him collect his soldiers. And he shared
        his grapes. Day two, they held hands

crossing Templeton Street. Today,
        she pours her brother juice. But he

doesn't want the juice, so he swings his arm
        widely, dumps the full cup on her lap.

His sister's kind act, he reports, *doesn't count.*
        She wails, *not fair.* The children retreat.

Their mother wrings the cloth,
        begins chopping the onions for dinner;

parsing the bulb as we do our children,
        with a rocking of the blade across the board.

Proper Burial

All morning, the storm.
Then worms, their bodies
juiced by the sun.

They litter our sidewalk.
My daughter collects them,
along with the browning

pink petals of the dogwood
dry-rivering the curb's edge.
How her small pile grows.

After lunch, she returns
to her work with a box
of tissues, and a plastic shovel.

From the dining room window, I watch her
first dig the hole, then awkwardly wrap
each tiny carcass in a shroud.
She stops to consider the muddy opening.

Our block's quiet houses consider
my daughter; her tossing
mummified worms into the air.

Resurrection of Dead Butterflies

The amateur collector captures a darting skipper
in his long-tailed net, then traps it
in a jar stuffed with tissues,
soaked in chemicals.

Though long dead,
Lorca, I wish that white gossamer
would hammer the glass,
slough off its rigor mortis.

It's possible one crack
is all anything needs
to be a fragmented glimmer
on a park bench after it rains.

It's hibernal solstice.

Don't you think this night is watchful
of its own specimens? It knows triumphs,
however brief, will find brightness
enough to spot the bend of the birch,
how it shelters small beasts.

I want the night to lift what's left
of the skipper's black-marked wings,

to take those torn strings and form
the sheen of constellations. Patterns

that will soothe this kept city, this suitcase
filled with figures made of felt and tin.

Nipple Reconstruction or No Nipple Reconstruction

Me: [Sitting shirtless on the papered plinth.]

Dr. V: *I had to ask am I*
asking the right questions?

Me: [Quiet as he rambles about his wife
dressing for a wedding, pasting adhesive
petals on her nipples. My husband
sitting in a plastic chair across the room.]

Dr. V: *So they won't show, she says to me. And I think*
why am I reconstructing nipples if a woman is only going to cover them?

Me: [Wondering if this is a rhetorical question,
and is this for real. Still shirtless. My husband
fiddling with his jacket's zipper.]

Dr. V: *I must say they're tricky, and don't hold up*
very well, but it's your decision, of course. There's
also the option of a 3D tattoo.

Me: [Feeling the sting, a sudden chill,
my one nipple rising.]

Laps

Today, my husband and I train easily side by   side,   within   the
borders. And though his broad-shouldered wake blinds me,   I know
how to glide past him just fine.   Then the frowning   woman   appears,
on the edge   scratches   my arm,   warning: I'm coming in.   Who
is she   to decide? This slow breaststroker. Politely, we share the makeshift
space, eight-feet wide. My husband passes her; she stops, she stands, protests,
Who do you think you are? He replies, tries to explain, but she retorts,   *our
President, too, thinks he knows what he's doing*. Pushing   off   the   wall,
I   kick   with   all   my   might.

Dear Mr. Bradbury,

I might've been that girl in your story,
the one her classmates locked in a closet

on a planet where the sun appears once
every seven years. How, at that exact moment,

they shut her away. Mr. Bradbury,
I realize it's possible I might've been the one

to lock her in. We're born mostly selfish.
As in, today, my youngest son gives the hermit crab

he's found to a girl who didn't have one,
while his brother hoards his in a tidal pool.

And yet, I think I've taught them just the same.
Mr. Bradbury, how remote I grow.

My Greatest Story

A great white shark beside me,
long and lean, not mean. At all.

Three times my size, and handsome.
I touch him, look

into the soundless loch of his eye.
Tell him, *You ain't no Jaws,*

though I shake inside.
Could punch him, but I like him—

his gliding fin, gills, teeth crowded in rows.
We move together until he's gone.

No one saw, so I
tell it to the plover, who tells

it to the tern—my story hovering
above the ocean, halfway

across the world; a girl
in Japan wondering if it's true.

I Have Many Concerns

Standing at the sink,
I poke the last scatter
of oats through the drain,
consider climbing in, as I might
back into the womb, weary
of what doom forbids.

My fears, pressed shin to
porcelain, hint of lemon
and mint. Suddenly, I'm soft
again, finding a home

within this war. Mineral
in smoke. Ashen cow.
Somewhere we hate each other,
and the children, colorful ants,
scamper beneath a chopper's blade.

Then what?

The ocean glistens the same everywhere.
Foil blankets. Human flow. Fear

breeds like the sac spider's eggs
laid in the corner of my bedroom.
I see the shape of its distortion,

how it arcs across the faucet's chrome.

College Break

My son's home,
sleeping in his old room.
The roses he picked
splay in a honey jar
on the sill above my desk.
He's making amends
for a heedless thing
he's done. The petals land
discreetly by the pens, then
all at once, they are a seam
of sequins pulled. And now,
they're clutter against the teak.
My son's gesture gone.
The browned edges cling
when I try to swipe them off.
They're troubling,
as if their falling
was shameful. No, not that.
As if it was messy. Closer.
I clear the strays,
linger over their broken
sheen. Weightless, soft,
still promising. Inevitable
as the young rain tumbling
on the bush outside.

Eggplants

In the yard, my neighbor Carol asks
why I love my husband,
with a thirst in her voice,
as if she's stranded,
and I have water.

I survey my husband;
how he bends over the garden stake;
the sight of his baring ass—two white eggplants—
its earthy and enduring crack.

Carol's unhappiness thrums
like the AC unit scolding the summer heat.

Easier when I could complain of my earlier divorce,
or the cording in my armpit from cancer.

When I sent my son to preschool,
a small mustard stain on his t-shirt,
she told me she felt better that day.

Her sadness domesticated, common
as the grackles prodding the feeder.

Carol studies me.

I look toward my husband,
him tending to the tangle of sugar snap peas.

Thinking of Adolph Gottlieb's *Drift* While I Mow the Grass

Someone threw the sun
into the sky. Its shrapnel

scatters the lawn, lands
in M.'s hair. No matter

what we say, light, acute
and unbounded, wants

to be heard, but who's willing
to know what the grass blades say?

M.'s arms are waving
as I ready the mower's throttle.

Beyond the engine's stridence,
his pantomime blurs.

So much goes unseen
when we can't hear. I think

the world's a silent movie.
Later, I find little suns

in my car, in plastic bottles
on my nightstand.

A Strand of Hair Found on the Shower Pane

My son, trapped by a storm,
first week away from home,
anchovied on a cot
in the campus center.

I slide this hair across
the window's steam
where it reveals its designs—

a question mark,

the Mother Mary's hood,

a hurricane's eye,

a pelican's beak.

No other choice. This homespun portent
is where I place my stock—

my fear's marrow,
my panic's marketplace.

To the Man at the Bus Stop

The way your sweater slouches,
how you lean against the city's maple,
tells me you know about waiting.
You pay no attention

to the six-pack of women gathered
at the stop, the kite string
of businessmen's ties, or
the mother's grip on her squirming son.
You observe the boy observing
an inchworm arching across the curb;

the boy picking the worm up
with a stick; the worm clinging to
the corrugated bark. I watch you
in your brown sweater watching
the bus peel in. When the mother
yanks the boy's arm, the stick drops.

I take my place on a plastic seat
and watch you through the window
searching the grass for the worm
still crossing the wood's all-too
terminable terrain. You're not
looking as we lumber away, but
bridging the stick to your finger.

I keep seeing you
in your brown, oversized sweater,
crouched near the ground.

When I arrive home, where the sea slopes
to our fence, I call to M., tell him *yes*,
but let's wait, let's be there

when the moon pulls in,
when the tide's crawling at our feet.

Early Morning Swim at Ballston Beach

My hand slips
between the currency.
O gold swell secure me.
What lurks
below is large
& though
quiet, looms
thick-skinned &
sinewy, seeking
fat to grab & thrash
for fuel, for temper.
I lost my wit for months;
one breast taken. A prefab
in its place; rigid,
scathing against the soft
scape of a heart abridged.
I'm more than half
full now & seasoned
with a coarse-cut salt. More
tender for the hunter, yes
but how else to exist
in this glide & thrust.
Terrified of any sharp thing
razoring my veins
yet unwilling to miss
the cold flush of this
wave. Apex predator,
how fast it arrows,
how exact it aims.

What I Want to Say Driving Home After My Mother's Check-Up

It's okay.   It's what we become;

a sepia tone same as the shadows
I've seen fall across Utah's red rock,
its striations glowing, baring those layers
polished by grim and pitiless erosion.

( )

I am your daughter, it seems
more glaring every day; my words
slipping, too. That look,
glazed, wonders where they are.

They're like the sleep that doesn't come,
or the morning paper. I'm missing you,
and your affirmative singular dots, all the while

my own ellipses pile, weightless thoughts.
Dear words, (mom let's pray):

Brave this mouth serrated, its grave
doubt.   Scars are acceptable.

( )

The audiologist adjusts her headphones,
tells her to repeat:

Say Talk   *Talk*
Say Hard   *Hard*
Say Dog   *Dog*
Say Bite   ___

Say Call   *Call*
Say Net   *Net*

( )

What we fear is travelling toward us.
But so is what we love; what is good,
and tender. You are my mother,

more palpable each day, you
reminisce, tell me again (dare I say)
of Mr. and Mrs. Honeybloom, your first apartment,
pushing the stroller downtown, and of when
I was young, in the backseat, hugging your shoulders
while you drove, we sang
Take Me Home, Country Roads.

( )

The fog persists.

Meaning anything
I say is questionable.

Not my eyes, not my ears,
not the window. But the fog.

I'm rehearsing what to say
but the fog forges my lines.
How to be understood?

A rattled burst of air strews
a small hole, enough, so if hunched
with chin jutted, I can spot
the exit sign in time.

Tea Ceremony

The Staffordshire teapot tips just so
when my mother's wrist bends,
emptying a flawless stream into
her cup. Steam surges, and the cat
she no longer bothers to usher off,
sleuths his tail between the rim
and handle. He settles his stripes
on the counter to stare down the jay
outside the window picking at
the suet cake. The stereo replaying
La Vie en Rose, the cat pretending
his stillness, gingersnaps,
poised on a plate. The kitchen's
stool urges me upright. My mother
reopens the cupboard, refolds
the checkered napkin, picks
lint off her lilac sweater.

Hard to Imagine Birds Dying of Old Age

My mother watches,
from the window, fixated

as a calico cat, perched on her suede chair,
the garland of robins on her magnolia tree;

the thing she says she'll miss the most
when she's gone. The birds delight

for hours. One day,
I trim the tree's branches but cut

too much. She cries,
then prays with *The Daily Word.*

I longed for her to sing
her songs in French again.

I wanted the sun
to have a chance,

to rouse those staid walls,
to leaven the raisin bread.

Lost and Found

Barren whelk shell—flesh,
warm and enviable, once. Whorled
scars ravish bleached calcium.

Is there a conspiracy? I ask my best friend who laughs too quickly.
We're walking along Priscilla Beach two weeks beyond my mastectomy.

The Atlantic, too, has a story spilling fast beneath its veneer—vast
current, forging this island where I nurse from stapled fruit.
Luckily my babies have grown.

This ductless wound
                    overflows.

Twenty years from now,
        will the knife hang
on a rafter, replaced by the nucleic;

will this shore find
        the clumps of trodden peat,
the battered shell intact?

Enough Means Plenty

I dig in the mudflats
for the soft shells, pious
as the white tulips by my fence
refusing to open, bodies clasped
inside the trap of themselves.

The stretched neck's tip, deep
in the bight, interrupts
the refined layers, spits
in protest. A match of wills
as it resists, burrows deeper,
an instinct for high tide.

I consider my thirst,
my hunger. How I never stop
pining for the warm lip of its salt.

Not Always Visible from a Vertical Position

Better seen when lying prone
on a hardwood floor. Blonde strands,

whisked together by household winds,
no longer tousled, or what Victorians wove

into their mourning. I've read *joy*
is not made to be a crumb,

nor is it meant to be a strand,
but perhaps a mane of iridescent thread,

longer than these collective lines,
lighter than the presumptive sky.

On the Occasion of Our Second Marriages

I pour the plaster then wait
for its hardening of lime and pumice.

I try to make permanent what the tide will
abolish then reshape with saltwater
dipped from the earth's clotted trough—

the necessary feeding for love's grave,
and altering motion.

For you, my groom,
I am framing my promise.

I wake early
to arrange, with two-by- fours, the sand flats,

> which at low tide, look like the loose lines
> of a nude splayed out for the moon

which pushes and pulls the ocean
across its particulate canvas—

> an awkward spine   a breast italicized,
two arms lounging   between folds

of finely crushed stones.   Or it's a tilled

New England field—fresh ruts streaming

from a horse's wobbling plow,

loamy blooms.

( )

At the studio, I spread clay
over and between the die's furrows;

     my fingertips roughened by grit's braille;
that I might find there the moon's model,

her held, though unfixable breath, or
     the brown foal's heaving flank.

Upward, I lift my bowl's edge, carefully
     temper its corners, also flare its base—

steadying this dedication,
grooved, and figurative, beautiful, and foolish,

     for as long as the world will allow.

Reconsidering the Oyster

Empty shell, purpled as a Georgia O'Keefe,
        in a puddle of ice.   I feel both hunger
            and horror for its raw absolute

as the walls of my throat encroach
        its slick descent.   I no longer
        taste the wine.   Still I pleasure.

For two weeks, the oyster, androgynous in its youth, floats
        before attaching,
        before pollinating a million spawn,
        before he turns she,
            spawning a million more.

It's three years before it's edible,
        before I appear from over the dunes,
to hunt, find, take;
           before I pry, split, eat.

I have that certain knife,
        curled at the tip,

           to break its hinge.

Acknowledgements

Thank you to Leah Maines, Christen Kincaid, and the staff at Finishing Line Press for making the publication of *Girl Without a Shirt,* my debut collection, possible.

I am thankful for Gigi Thibodeau, my first poetry mentor, who knew when to push me out of the nest into Lesley University's MFA program, where I met Erin Belieu, who taught me how to write beyond the stretch of my hand. Much gratitude for her, and all the faculty for opening new pathways.

Love to my poet-mates with a special shout-out to Sarah Lain and Eileen Cleary for their contagious energy and unwavering support. Thank you to Kevin McLellan for his multiple readings and guidance, and to his workshop mates for their feedback and encouragement; to Kathy Nilsson and Michael Mercurio for their earlier readings of the manuscript, and to Martha McCollough for her help in the cover art's layout and design.

Special thanks to Erin Belieu, Martha Collins, and Rhina P. Espaillat for their thoughtful reading and support.

I am grateful for Carlene Carrabino, my dearest friend, who travelled with me across the country three decades ago, sharing a jeep, a tent, and a jug of water, and who always makes me laugh.

For my siblings, my memorable childhood, and for my parents Don & Rachel, for being my greatest listeners and biggest cheerleaders, who taught me how to be *up and grateful.*

For my children, Megan & Owen, who have taught (and keep teaching) me more than ever imaginable. Also, for Elka & Katarina for opening their hearts.

And for Michael, the true love of my trinity, along with poetry and saltwater. I am grateful for every day together. Without him, this book (and its vibrant cover art) would not exist.

Notes

This manuscript has worn many titles, but it wasn't until I was sitting in the plastic surgeon's office, shirtless, that *Girl Without a Shirt* found its voice. I realized not wearing a shirt represented many stages of my life: from early childhood, running shirtless in the yard with my brothers, to motherhood, nursing my child, to becoming a breast cancer survivor, and everything in between. *Girl Without a Shirt* represents my innocence, my sexuality, my vulnerability, and my courage.

"Again, I Take to the Trees": The line, *a feeling confessing itself to itself* is derived from John Stuart Mill's "Essay on Poetry."

"A Strand of Hair Curled Like a Nautilus on a Page of Rumi": *Eadem mutata resurgo* is a Latin phrase that literally translates to "Although changed, I arise the same" or "I rise again changed but the same." The phrase was first known to be used by Jakob Bernoulli, a member of the famous Swiss mathematical family, and appears on his tombstone in Basel.

"DaVinci's Treatise *On Painting*": Inspired by a remark in Leonardo DaVinci's book *On Painting* claiming his paintings could "make a dog bark."

"Swimming, Dark Like": The reference to the portraits, "a smile like her mother's" derived from the poem, "Double-Image," by Anne Sexton.

"What Do We, Failing, Know of Virtue?": Based on the painting, *Renaissance Dream Drawing: Shores of Time* by Nancy Ellen Craig (1927-2015). Nancy was a friend of mine and Michael. We cooked and shared many meals together at her home in Truro, MA.

"Resurrection of Dead Butterflies": The title comes from a line in Federico Garcia Lorca's poem, "Sleepless City (Brooklyn Bridge Nocturne)."

"Dear Mr. Bradbury,": Inspired by Ray Bradbury's short story *All Summer in a Day*.

"I Have Many Concerns": Some of the imagery presented is inspired by Ai Weiwei's documentary *Human Flow*.

"Thinking of Adolph Gotlieb's *Drift* While I Mow the Grass": Refers to Adolph Gotlieb's painting *Drift*, 1961, exhibited at The Fogg Art Museum, Harvard University.

"Not Always Visible from a Vertical Position": The line *joy is not made to be a crumb*, is from the poem 'Don't Hesitate" by Mary Oliver.

Christine Jones lives on Cape Cod, with her husband, where you'll find them swimming and surfing in their shark-mitigating wetsuits. She earned her MFA from Lesley University in Cambridge, Massachusetts, and is a therapist and mother of two. She's founder/editor-in-chief of *Poems2go,* an international public poetry project, and an associate editor of *Lily Poetry Review.* Her poems have appeared in numerous journals and online, including *32 poems, cagibi, Passager Books, Sugar House Review, Blue Mountain Review, Ruminate, Mom Egg Review, Literary Mama, Salamander;* also broadcasted on WOMR's Poet's Corner, and WCAI"s Poetry Sunday. This is her debut poetry book.